Warning

Jonah

by Andrew Reid

MATTHIAS MEDIA

Warning Signs
© Andrew Reid, 2002.

Matthias Media
PO Box 225
Kingsford NSW 2032 Australia
Ph: (02) 9663 1478
Fax: (02) 9663 3265
Email: info@matthiasmedia.com.au
Internet: www.matthiasmedia.com.au

Distributed in the United Kingdom by:
The Good Book Company
Ph: (020) 8942 0880
Fax: (020) 8942 0990
Email: admin@thegoodbook.co.uk
Internet: www.thegoodbook.co.uk

Distributed in South Africa by:
Christian Book Discounters
Ph: (021) 685 3663
Email: peter@christianbooks.co.za

ISBN 1 876326 44 1

Cover design and typesetting by Joy Lankshear Design.
St Matthias Press Ltd. ACN 067 558 365

Contents

Other Interactive and Topical Bible Studies from Matthias Media:

Our Interactive Bible Studies (IBS) and Topical Bible Studies (TBS) are a valuable resource to help you keep feeding from God's Word. The IBS series works through passages and books of the Bible; the TBS series pulls together the Bible's teaching on topics, such as money or prayer. As at April 2002, the series contains the following titles:

BEYOND EDEN
(GENESIS 1-11)
Authors: Phillip Jensen and
Tony Payne, 9 studies

THE ONE AND ONLY
(DEUTERONOMY)
Author: Bryson Smith,
8 studies

THE GOOD, THE BAD & THE UGLY
(JUDGES)
Author: Mark Baddely,
10 studies

FAMINE & FORTUNE
(RUTH)
Authors: Barry Webb and
David Hohne, 4 studies

THE EYE OF THE STORM
(JOB)
Author: Bryson Smith,
6 studies

THE SEARCH FOR MEANING
(ECCLESIASTES)
Author: Tim McMahon,
9 studies

TWO CITIES
(ISAIAH)
Authors: Andrew Reid and
Karen Morris, 9 studies

KINGDOM OF DREAMS
(DANIEL)
Authors: Andrew Reid and
Karen Morris, 8 studies

BURNING DESIRE
(OBADIAH & MALACHI)
Authors: Phillip Jensen and
Richard Pulley, 6 studies

FULL OF PROMISE
(THE BIG PICTURE OF THE O.T.)
Authors: Phil Campbell
and Bryson Smith, 8 studies

THE GOOD LIVING GUIDE
(MATTHEW 5:1-12)
Authors: Phillip Jensen and
Tony Payne, 9 studies

NEWS OF THE HOUR
(MARK)
Author: Peter Bolt, 10 studies

FREE FOR ALL
(GALATIANS)
Authors: Phillip Jensen
and Kel Richards, 8 studies

WALK THIS WAY
(EPHESIANS)
Author: Bryson Smith,
8 studies

THE COMPLETE CHRISTIAN
(COLOSSIANS)
Authors: Phillip Jensen and
Tony Payne, 8 studies

TO THE HOUSEHOLDER
(1 TIMOTHY)
Authors: Phillip Jensen and
Greg Clarke, 9 studies

RUN THE RACE
(2 TIMOTHY)
Author: Bryson Smith,
6 studies

THE PATH TO GODLINESS
(TITUS)
Authors: Phillip Jensen and
Tony Payne, 6 studies

FROM SHADOW TO REALITY
(HEBREWS)
Author: Joshua Ng, 10 studies

THE IMPLANTED WORD
(JAMES)
Authors: Phillip Jensen and
K.R. Birkett, 8 studies

HOMEWARD BOUND
(1 PETER)
Authors: Phillip Jensen and
Tony Payne, 10 studies

ALL YOU NEED TO KNOW
(2 PETER)
Author: Bryson Smith,
6 studies

BOLD I APPROACH
(PRAYER)
Author: Tony Payne, 6 studies

CASH VALUES
(MONEY)
Author: Tony Payne, 5 studies

THE BLUEPRINT
(DOCTRINE)
Authors: Phillip Jensen
and Tony Payne, 11 studies

WOMAN OF GOD
(THE BIBLE ON WOMEN)
Authors: Terry Blowes
8 studies

How to make the most of these studies

1. What is an Interactive Bible Study?

These 'interactive' Bible studies are a bit like a guided tour of a famous city. The studies will take you through Jonah, pointing out things along the way, filling in background details, and suggesting avenues for further exploration. But there is also time for you to do some sight-seeing of your own—to wander off, have a good look for yourself, and form your own conclusions.

In other words, we have designed these studies to fall half-way between a sermon and a set of unadorned Bible study questions. We want to provide stimulation and input and point you in the right direction, while leaving you to do a lot of the exploration and discovery yourself.

We hope that these studies will stimulate lots of 'interaction'—interaction with the Bible, with the things we've written, with your own current thoughts and attitudes, with other people as you discuss them, and with God as you talk to him about it all.

2. The format

Each study contains sections of text to introduce, summarize, suggest and provoke. We've left plenty of room in the margins for you to jot comments and questions as you read. Interspersed throughout the text are two types of 'interaction', each with their own symbol:

For starters

Questions to break the ice and get you thinking.

Investigate

Questions to help you investigate key parts of the Bible.

Think it through

Questions to help you think through the implications of your discoveries and write down your own thoughts and reactions.

When you come to one of these symbols, you'll know that it's time to do some work of your own.

3. Suggestions for Individual Study

- Before you begin, pray that God would open your eyes to what he is saying in his Word and give you the spiritual strength to do something about it. You may be spurred to pray again at the end of the study.
- Work through the study, following the directions as you go. Write in the spaces provided.
- Resist the temptation to skip over the *Think it through* sections. It is important to think about the sections of text (rather than just accepting them as true) and to ponder the implications for your life. Writing these things down is a very valuable way to get your thoughts working.
- Take what opportunities you can to talk to others about what you've learnt.

4. Suggestions for Group Study

- Much of the above applies to group study as well. The studies are suitable for structured Bible study or cell groups, as well as for more informal pairs and threesomes. Get together with a friend/s and work through them at your own pace; use them as the basis for regular Bible study with your spouse. You don't need the formal structure of a 'group' to gain maximum benefit.

- It is *vital* that group members work through the study themselves *before* the group meets. The group discussion can take place comfortably in an hour (depending on how side-tracked you get!), but only if all the members have done the work and are familiar with the material.

- Spend most of the group time discussing the 'interactive' sections—*Investigate* and *Think it through.* Reading all the text together will take too long and should be unnecessary if the group members have done their preparation. You may wish to underline and read aloud particular paragraphs or sections of text that you think are important.

- The role of the group leader is to direct the course of the discussion and to try to draw the threads together at the end. This will mean a little extra preparation—underlining important sections of text to emphasize, working out which questions are worth concentrating on, and being sure of the main thrust of the study. Leaders will also probably want to work out approximately how long they'd like to spend on each part.

- We haven't included an 'answer guide' to the questions in the studies. This is a deliberate move. We want to give you a guided tour, not a lecture. There is more than enough in the text we have written and the questions we have asked to point you in what we think is the right direction. The rest is up to you.

The rebellious prophet

For starters

What do you already know about the book of Jonah?

The modern city of Tel Aviv lies on the eastern shore of the Mediterranean, some thirty miles from Jerusalem. Within this modern city are the ruins of a famous ancient city—the seaport of Joppa. In biblical history, Joppa was renowned as the port where Solomon landed his great cedars from Lebanon (2 Chr 2:16) and for its connection with two very famous reluctant missionaries to the Gentiles. In Acts 9-11, we are told that it was in Joppa that Peter was prepared by God through a vision to change his attitude to Gentile uncleanness. This preparation opened him to the otherwise incomprehensible possibility that he should go to the household of the Gentile Cornelius to preach the gospel. Cornelius became the first Gentile convert to Christianity.

In the book of Jonah, Joppa is the location from which the prophet Jonah made his bid to escape from the command and presence of God in a ship bound for Tarshish (Jonah 1:1-3).

The book of Jonah does not say when the events recorded actually happened. One clue can be found in the fact that the book is set at a time when the city of Nineveh was large and significant on the world stage. Another comes from the only other reference we have in the Bible to a prophet by the name of 'Jonah, son of Amittai'—in 2 Kings 14:25—who prophesied during the reign of Jeroboam II (approximately 782-753 BC). This general time frame does coincide with a time in which Nineveh was probably flourishing as the capital city of the then leading world power, the Assyrians. Some of the famous references to Assyria and Nineveh in the Bible apart from the book of Jonah include Isaiah 7:17-25, Isaiah 36-38, 2 Kings 17, and the prophecies of Nahum and Zephaniah.

The prophecies of Nahum and Zephaniah indicate that the city of Nineveh was not viewed positively by the nation of Israel. It represented everything that was big, bad, arrogant and an intolerable affront to God. It was a great and evil city at the head of a godless nation that severely threatened the people of God. It is this city that Jonah is told to go and preach against in Jonah 1.

Investigate

Read the following Old Testament passages: Jonah 1:1-3; Exodus 3:1-4:17; Isaiah 6 and Jeremiah 1:1-10. (These passages record God calling some key prophets to their ministry.)

1. Compare the way Jonah interacts with God in Jonah 1:1-3 with the way Moses, Isaiah, and Jeremiah interact with God in the other passages. How is it the same? How is it different?

2. Look up the following verses and see what you can discover from them about Tarshish. Why do you think Jonah may have chosen Tarshish as the place to which he would flee?

• 2 Chronicles 9:21

• Isaiah 66:19

Jonah and the mariners

In this section of the study we will explore the rest of chapter 1 from the perspective of Jonah and the mariners. Before getting underway we need to note some important facts about each of the parties involved.

First, Jonah is a Jew. He is therefore clearly one of God's people. Like many Jews he probably viewed the sea with some trepidation. Apart from a few people who were sailors or fishermen, most Jews appear to have been landlubbers, who viewed the sea as a place of dark sea monsters, where chaotic forces were at work and where waves heaved and rolled (cf. Ps 107:23-32). Nevertheless, Jonah obviously considered travelling westward on the dark and dangerous sea with Gentile mariners to a land where God was unknown and not honoured a much better option than God's proposed alternative—travelling toward Nineveh in the presence of God and bearing the word of God.

Second, the mariners are apparently experienced sailors. However, they are not Jews and therefore outsiders. They know nothing of Jonah's God, and they do not know that Jonah is fleeing him. When Jonah arrives at their boat, they apparently regard him as simply another normal passenger.

Third, God is the Creator of the heavens, the sea, and the dry land (Jonah 1:9, Ps 104-105). There is no place on earth where his influence is not felt or his control not exercised. As he who walks "in the recesses of the deep" (Job 38:16), he can use the wind and the waves for his purposes, which is what he does here in his pursuit of Jonah and his obedience.

It is also important to understand the idea of "the fear of the LORD" in the Old Testament. It is a somewhat technical term that means to tremble before God as God, that is, to respect and revere him. Such fear was not just an attitude but resulted in action. Hence, people who 'feared God' expressed their fear by listening to his word, obeying him and serving him.

Investigate

Read Jonah 1:4-17.

1. Note down the different attitudes of the Mariners and Jonah to:

The storm
  Mariners

  Jonah

The gods/God
  Mariners

  Jonah

2. Find all references to 'fear' or being afraid in the passage (the same Hebrew word lies behind each reference). Who claims to fear God and who expresses that fear appropriately?

In his closing words to the Jews in Acts 7:51ff, Stephen says that his listeners are just like their forefathers in that they are "stiff-necked people, uncircumcised in heart and ears, and always resisting the Holy Spirit". The sense is that they had the outward signs of being God's people but their hearts were far from being sensitive to God and his word.

One of the great tragedies of this first chapter of Jonah is that the outsiders—the mariners—come out looking so much better than Jonah, who had access to God in his word. However, instead of embracing God and his word with fear, joy and enthusiasm, Jonah is found running when God speaks, sleeping when God acts in the storm, and sulking when God acts in mercy according to his character (Jonah 4).

We see similar things happen in the New Testament in the Gospels and Acts. For example, Mark records for us in his Gospel that the Jews are resistant, the disciples somewhat uncomprehending, and the outsiders the most responsive. Paul's missionary journeys are full of the record of his frustration with speaking the gospel to Jews who largely respond with jealousy and persecution.

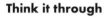

Think it through

1. Choose one of these situations that you have experienced yourself or seen others experience:
- A time when a person first caught a glimpse of God's holiness and their own sinfulness.
- An occasion when God's word about Jesus came to someone with full conviction (e.g. through reading the Bible or hearing it preached).
- A time of reading God's word when it became clear that he wanted you to change your life or actions in some way in response to his word.

Note: If you are working through this study with a group of people, you might like to share some of these events with others.

2. What are the different ways you have responded to God's commands? Is/was your response more like that of Jonah or that of the mariners?

3. How do you respond to God when in the company of outsiders? Is there anything to be ashamed of before God and them?

4. There is a deep tragedy in Jonah 1. However, the tragedy is far greater for those of us who have heard God's living word in Jesus and rejected it or regarded it with complacency. Can we be too quick to condemn Jonah? Spend some time praying about your own attitude to God and his word, that of your congregation, and that of the wider Christian community where you live.

2

A great Old Testament word

For starters

Do you find it hard to believe that God is loving and kind? Why/why not?

Throughout the Old Testament, there are a number of passages where God clearly declares his nature to his people. One of the grandest of these passages is Exodus 34:6-7 where God reveals himself to Moses and proclaims to him these words:

> The LORD, the LORD, a God merciful and gracious, slow to anger, and abounding in steadfast love and faithfulness, keeping steadfast love for thousands, forgiving iniquity and transgression and sin, but who will by no means clear the guilty, visiting the iniquity of the fathers on the children and the children's children, to the third and the fourth generation.

Behind the two references to 'steadfast love' stands one Hebrew word: *hesed.* This word is translated in a variety of ways in our English translations of the Bible, such as, 'mercy', 'lovingkindness', 'goodness', 'favour' and 'love'. It is one of the favourite words used within the Old Testament to describe God's character and actions toward his people, and probably lies behind such important words as 'grace' and 'love' in the New Testament. It is also a word that is used in two crucial passages within the book of Jonah: Jonah 2:8 and 4:2. Because it is so important, we are going to take a short diversion from our studies in Jonah to try and get some background information on this word so that we can better appreciate its use when we come to it within the book of Jonah.

Given that Jonah's use of *hesed* in Jonah 4:2 has distinct echoes of Exodus 34:6-7 it makes sense to start there and to see if the context of these verses helps us understand what it means there.

Investigate

Read Exodus 32:1-34:9

1. It is clear that the sin of Israel depicted in this passage is great, deliberate and provocative. Is there any indication of repentance within the passage?

2. What is God's initial response and what is his proposed long-term response? Would such a response have been justified (cf. Exodus 20:4-5)?

3. Does God carry out the sorts of response indicated by Exodus 20:4-5? According to Exodus 32-34, what stops him carrying out his long-term response?

The God of *hesed*

The story of the Old Testament is one which clearly indicates that although God had been faithful to his people, they had been grossly unfaithful to him. He had been a lover of his people but they responded to his love by acting like prostitutes and going off after other gods (e.g. Hos 1-3; Jer 2; Ezek 16). They had continually broken the covenant that existed between them and God, and it was recognised by the prophets that God would have been entirely justified in walking away from the relationship.

Passages such as Micah 7:18-20 celebrate that God did not do the justified thing (the word *hesed* stands behind 'steadfast love' in verses 18 and 20). Instead, he acted in surprising and unobligated mercy, kindness and love. As he did in Exodus 32-34, he "relented" and had compassion, treading down iniquity under his foot and casting sins into the depths of the sea.

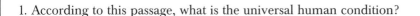

Investigate

Read Romans 3:9-31.

1. According to this passage, what is the universal human condition?

2. Given that God is holy, what would be his entirely justified response?

3. How does God act in response to the universal human condition, and what is his mechanism for this?

The New Testament is clear that the nature of God has not changed between the Testaments. He is still holy and he still punishes sin. However, his mercy and love (*hesed*) triumphs over judgement. God is able to be "just" and the "justifier of him who has faith in Jesus".

In other words, the New Testament records for us how it is that God is able to 'relent' or 'change his mind' about exercising judgement on those who truly deserve it. He does not do it by simply forgetting about sin. Rather, he turns his anger toward sin upon himself by allowing his sinless Son to take the punishment due for our sinfulness.

One passage in the New Testament that eloquently captures the nature of God's *hesed* is the parable of the lost son in Luke 15. This parable and the accompanying parables of the lost sheep and the lost coin were told in response to the Pharisees and teachers of the law who were critical of Jesus welcoming sinners and eating with them. The parable of the lost son shows a father who is overflowing in his love for the son who has strayed. This love goes far beyond duty and obligation. It also goes far beyond commonly accepted norms of behaviour, and far beyond the expectations the son might have had of him. It is spontaneous, unexpected, unmerited, overflowing love and grace. It is *hesed*.

Think it through

Read Luke 15:1-32.

1. In essence, what is it that the Pharisees and the older son were grumbling about?

2. The nature of God's grace is that it is by definition not merited or earned. It is clear that a number of people in the New Testament found this a significant sticking point in their acceptance of the gospel. Why do you think we find God's grace objectionable in this way?

3. Can you think of any ways in which people act or speak that indicate that they find God's *hesed* difficult or objectionable?

4. In what ways do you find God's *hesed* a difficult concept? Why?

5. What great comforts can we find in God's *hesed?*

A song from the deep

For starters

At what points in your life have you been very conscious of God's mercy towards you?

The book of Jonah is markedly different in style from the other minor prophets of the Old Testament. Where they focus on the sayings of the prophet, the book of Jonah focuses on what happened to the prophet and on his reaction to these things.

This, along with a number of other characteristics found within the book, has led some people in recent times to ask whether this book is really history. They have suggested that instead of history it may be a form of fiction (e.g. allegory, parable, prophetic parable, satire, short story).

The major arguments proposed in favour of fiction are:
- The historical improbability of some of the events to modern readers (e.g. rescue by a great fish, repentance of the entire city, remarkable growth of the plant).
- The use of hyperbole (everything is supposedly exaggerated, such as the size of the city and of the fish).
- The clear evidence of design and symmetry in the book's structure (said to be more characteristic of an imaginative product than careful and straightforward historical writing).

The major arguments in favour of history are:
- Most commentators up until relatively recently have viewed the book as historical and the events depicted in it as having actually occurred. They were convinced that Jonah was not intending to write fiction. For example, Josephus, writing in the first century, counts the story of Jonah as of the same sort of writing as other books depicting the history of the Jews. Ancient authorities are likely to be more dependable, as they are more likely to be familiar with the genre of their own day and how to comprehend it.
- It is strange to tie the book into the life of a specific historical character if the book is entirely fictional.
- The events described in the book are not unlike those described elsewhere in the history books of the Old Testament (e.g. the ministry of Elijah in 1 Kings 17-19).

An inherent problem with the first approach is that it comes with an assumption—that the miraculous and/or the supernatural can never happen and therefore the book must be fictional, greatly embellished or simply wrong. If however, you are a believer in the God who is presented in Jonah 1—the God of heaven who created the sea and the dry land—then you believe that God can do anything he chooses. You are then somewhat free to examine the book as it presents itself. As we do this, we can agree with the ancient interpreters whose view about God was somewhat akin to ours. That is, we can read it as the story of a particular set of circumstances in the life of a Jewish prophet that has been recorded and incorporated into the word of God because of the key things those events teach about God and his way of working in his world.

Investigate

Read Jonah 1:17-2:10.

1. List the key things Jonah says about God in his 'psalm'.

2. At what point in the psalm does Jonah say that his attitude to God changed? What caused this change? How does God respond to this change?

3. The verb 'to save' literally means 'to deliver or rescue from things that confine or constrain'. Read the following passages from the Old Testament that talk about God saving people. In each case, write down what it is that God saves *from*.

   Exodus 14:13 (cf. 15:2)

   2 Samuel 3:18

   Job 5:15

   Isaiah 38:20 (cf. verse 9)

   Ezekiel 34:22

4. In what way has Jonah experienced salvation? What has he been saved from?

Remembering the God of *hesed*

In our last study we examined the idea of God's *hesed*. We saw that the word was used to describe the nature of God to act in spontaneous, unobligated and often unexpected mercy and grace. The father in the parable of the lost son in Luke 15 demonstrates what God is like by going beyond all the norms of expected behaviour and rushing out to meet his son and bring him home.

Our reason for examining this word was because it appears in two crucial passages within the book of Jonah. The first one of these passages is Jonah 2. Unfortunately some of our versions of the Bible have so translated the passage that it is not immediately apparent that the word does occur. However, some of the more literal translations of the Bible, such as the English Standard Version, have done us the favour of using the same phrase ('steadfast love') to translate *hesed* in Exodus 34:6, Jonah 2:8 and Jonah 4:2. The ESV translates Jonah 2:8 in this fashion: "Those who pay regard to vain idols forsake their hope of steadfast love".

The God revealed in the Old Testament therefore offers something that no other God offers—he is the God who is merciful and gracious, slow to anger and abounding in steadfast love and faithfulness. He is the God who can 'relent' from bringing disaster (Exod 32:14; 1 Chr 21:15; Amos 7:6). He can act in such a way that his mercy triumphs over judgement (Jas 2:13). This is the God we see acting in the death of Jesus in the New Testament, not giving us what we deserve but what we need. Jonah's point is that those who cling to worthless idols are missing out on something they desperately need. As the NIV puts it, they forfeit the grace that could be theirs.

Think it through

1. Re-read Jonah 1. In what way are the mariners and Jonah similar in:

• their experiences?

• their responses to God?

• their experience of God?

2. If you were to find a verse in Jonah 1-2 that summarises the two chapters, which would it be? Why would you choose this verse?

3. What point do you think the author might wish to make in describing the experiences of the mariners and Jonah in such similar ways?

4. In what way does the book of Jonah point us toward some great New Testament truths? (You might like to have a look at the following passages—John 10:16; Acts 10-11; Ephesians 2:11-22).

The repentance of Nineveh

For starters

What are the indications of true repentance in a person's life?

As we have seen in our previous studies, the book of Jonah is full of God's gracious and steadfast love. This theme is apparent yet again in Jonah 3:1 when we are told that "The word of the Lord came to Jonah a second time". Scripture often records that "the word of the Lord came to" someone. Here however, we are told it came to a particular prophet "a second time".

As one who had been given such a great responsibility and who had so clearly been an open rebel against God, he deserved nothing but God's judgement (cf. the "man of God" of 1 Kings 13 who died because of his disobedience). However, God does not act as Jonah deserves. God shows mercy and forgiveness in not discarding his disobedient prophet, and takes him up again for the most important task that God can give—to speak the word of God.

Clearing the ground

Before we get down to having a look at the details of the passage, it will be helpful to clear the ground a bit. In this regard, verse 3 clearly holds a few statements that need clarification. First, there is the reference to the time that a visit took. Although Nineveh was undoubtedly a large city (Jonah 4:11 tells us that 120,000 people lived there), the three days probably refers not to the time it took to walk from one side to the other but the time it took for all the proper ancient protocols of such a major city to be observed. Alternatively, the phrase could imply that a prophetic visit took three days because it needed to ensure that the message was heard by the bulk of the population.

Second, the English Standard Version of the Bible records an alternative translation for the phrase "an exceedingly great city". It can more literally be rendered "a great city to God". One commentator on the passage translates these words as 'a city great to God' or 'a city important to God'. The point of such a translation is that this was a city whose size was not the issue but its importance in relation to God. It is a city God is concerned for. This is stressed in Jonah 4, much to Jonah's dismay.

Investigate

Read Jonah 3:1-8

1. What do we know about the city of Nineveh from the book of Jonah itself (cf. Jonah 1:2; 3:2-3; 4:11)?

2. Nineveh was a '3 day visit city'. How long did it take before Jonah began to get a response?

3. Read Jeremiah 18:7-10. Although this was written some time after Jonah's time, it appears to provide a pattern for God's interaction with a pagan nation. List the elements of that pattern in terms of what the nation does and what God does.

4. How does the Judaean king, Jehoiakim, respond to the prophetic word in Jeremiah 36:9-31? How does the King of Nineveh respond in Jonah 3?

Jehoiakim

The King of Nineveh

Another example for God's people

In his letter to the Romans, the apostle Paul indicates that Jews have a greater responsibility before God because they have been entrusted with the oracles of God (Rom 3:2). They know God's will and purpose through his word and should therefore know how to live before and with God. Moreover, they should know just how far they fall short of God's demands. Unfortunately, the history of God's people in the Old Testament was that they often sinned with a high hand, and were either pitifully unaware of their sinfulness or simply chose to ignore it.

Israelite history up to this point had been tainted by many great acts of corporate sinfulness. However, there had never been an act of corporate repentance anything like the one we see here by the Ninevites. Just as the mariners had put God's man, Jonah, to shame in chapter 1, so the Ninevites put God's people to shame here and show them the way ahead.

Having said this, it is important to note what is going on here. Just as the repentance of the pagan Nebuchadnezzar in the book of Daniel does not appear to suggest his conversion, so it is here. Moreover, the repentance did not endure either, since Nineveh continued to be a nation noted for its great evil. What did happen here was that when God confronted them at this particular point in their history, they showed genuine and apparently heartfelt contrition. This was enough for God to do as he had done often enough with his own people—relent from sending calamity, even though sin was all so quickly renewed.

Investigate

1. What is the catalyst for the repentance of the Ninevites?

2. What are the signs of repentance that are displayed by the Ninevites in the following areas:

   • How they thought

   • What they said

   • How they acted

3. Are there any indications within the text as to why they repented as they did? What are these indications?

4. Read the following passages that describe repentance or acts of repentance. Put together a 'profile' of a repentant person from one or all of these passages. If you are doing this study in a group you might like to split the group members into twos or threes, with each group looking at one passage.

2 Kings 22-23

Ezra 9-10

Daniel 9:1-19

Luke 18:9-14

Jonah 3 began by saying that the word of the Lord came to Jonah. Daniel's repentance in Daniel 9 similarly begins with his meditation upon Scripture. Did you notice how many of the acts of repentance in the passages above were connected with the reading of Scripture or the hearing of God's word pronounced? This is where godly repentance begins, because in the word of God we hear who God is and what we are like. It is this that brings us to our knees. This is why repentance is a key element in becoming a Christian—it is when we hear what we are like, and how rich in mercy God has been toward us despite our sin.

In 2 Corinthians 7:5-13, Paul describes the repentance of a group of Christians. He remarks that their repentance was marked by such things as grief, lack of regret at having to turn from sin, indignation, zeal, determination, eagerness and punishment. This latter sort of repentance is the sort that should characterize the people of God at all times, not just at special events. When God's word convicts us of sin, righteousness and judgement as it inevitably will, our repentance should be this godly grief that results in actions.

Think it through

1. Think back to the last time that you heard or read God's word and were confronted by your need to change your thinking or actions. How did you react? That is,

• How did you think?

• What did you say (even if it was only to yourself or God)?

• How did your actions change as a result?

2. If you have not felt convicted by the need to change for some time, why do you think this might be and what can you do about it?

3. Write down some practical steps you might take to help yourself and others to follow through better on repentance and to make it more enduring.

Jonah 3:10 – 4:11

Why is Jonah angry with God?

For starters

What does it feel like to be excluded from a group? What does it feel like to then be included?

The Bible is full of walls—real ones, and metaphorical ones. A wall represents a division between two people or places, a barrier which prevents them being united. Walls keep people apart. And the removal of walls—like the fall of the Berlin Wall in 1989—is a very powerful symbol for bringing people back together again.

The Bible begins with God's vision for a world without walls. His world will be a place where humans live in right relationship with God, with each other and with the environment in which he has placed them to live. God's dream for humanity is about a place with no walls between God and humans, humans and each other, and humans and the world they live in.

However, within fifty or so short verses this dream lies shattered. The ideal has gone and the first bricks have been laid in a series of walls between:

i. God and people (Adam and his wife and their descendants are locked out of the presence of God);

ii. people and other people (Cain murders his brother); and

iii. people and the environment (the land bears thistles and thorns).

The Old Testament goes on to tell us that God has not forgotten his ideal. On the contrary, he works to bring about a return to Eden. However, the way he does it seems strange. He starts to erect his own 'wall' around his people. Although he does have the good of the whole world in mind, he brings about this good by separating one nation from all others and calling it 'special'. This separation is heightened by the giving of the law in Exodus 19-20. There are but a few little breaches through the walls to let strangers in—Rahab the prostitute, Ruth the Moabite, and the Gibeonites of Joshua 9.

By the time of Jesus, this sense of separation is extreme. Inside the walls are God's people—the ones to whom God has made himself known and who therefore have access to the God of the whole earth. Outside the walls are the rest, variously known as the Gentiles, the Nations, and other less complimentary names. They are without God and therefore without hope in the world (Eph 2:12).

If you were to take a guided tour of Herod's temple at the time of Christ, you would see this division up close. The building was a magnificent structure sitting atop an elevated platform and symbolising the presence of God. Around the temple were a number of courts for the priests, ordinary male Jews and ordinary female Jews. As you approached this platform, there was a wall at ground level. If you were to approach this wall as a Gentile, you would be confronted by a sign written in Greek and Latin that read:

> No foreigner may enter within the barrier and enclosure round the temple. Anyone who is caught doing so will have himself to blame for his ensuing death.

Jews of the first century and many of their predecessors from previous centuries held this mindset. They were the special people of God and all others were outsiders and not worthy of God's concern, interest and grace.

Some of this mindset is apparent in the book of Jonah.

Investigate

Read Jonah 3:10-4:4

1. Jonah 3:10 literally reads: "God relented of the disaster that he had said he would do to them, and he did not do it" (ESV). What light does the immediate context throw on the meaning of 'relent' here?

2. The statement that God relented can be found in a number of other key passages in the Old Testament. What does it appear to mean in them?

2 Samuel 24:10-17

Joel 2:12-14

Jeremiah 18:7-10

Jonah 4:2

3. No explanation is given in Jonah 1 as to what motivated Jonah's disobedience. What's is Jonah's own explanation in Jonah 4?

4. Why is Jonah angry in Jonah 4?

Walls coming down

Joel 2 is strikingly similar in its language to Jonah 3 and 4. Both talk about people 'turning' or 'returning', and of repentance shown in people's hearts and actions. Both passages talk about God 'relenting', and both are heavily dependent upon Exodus 34:6-7 and the surrounding story of God's relenting over Israel's sin.

There is a difference however, between these Old Testament passages and Jonah 4. The other passages speak about God 'relenting' from sending disaster upon his own people. Jonah knew that mercy was at the very core of God's being because God had done this so often with his own people. If it was at the core of God's being, then Jonah's great fear was that the walls God appeared to have erected around his people would not restrain it. Jonah feared that God would act according to his nature and forgive outsiders in the same way that he forgave his own people. To Jonah this was scandalous.

The New Testament describes God's systematic demolishing of the walls that had been in place for so long. In the death of Jesus we see the walls obliterated—both the wall which separates sinful humanity from God, and the wall which separates Jew from Gentile.

Even before his death, in the ministry of Jesus, we see cracks appear in the wall between Jews and others. The Book of Acts spells out in more detail the way in which Christ's death brought down that wall, culminating in the conversion of the Roman centurion, Cornelius, in Acts 10-11. As Paul puts it in Ephesians 2, the dividing wall of hostility came crashing down (Eph 2:11-22) because of the death of Jesus on behalf of *all.*

Investigate

Read Jonah 4:5-11. The context for Jonah 4:5-11 is set by Jonah 3:10-4:4, particularly verse 4, where we are told that Jonah is angry and where God asks if Jonah's anger is right.

1. How does Jonah express his anger?

2. Does the passage give us any insight into the justification for his anger? What is that justification?

3. How does God *act* in response to Jonah's anger?

4. What does God *say* in response to Jonah's anger?

5. Summarise the point that God is making using the plant.

Think it through

Read Matthew 18:21-35.

1. What similarities are there between Jonah and the unforgiving servant?

2. What is the essential sin committed by the unforgiving servant?

3. This passage gives one way in which we can be like Jonah. In what other ways can we as Christians be like Jonah?

4. How do such attitudes express themselves in our thinking and acting?

5. What consolation can we draw from the book of Jonah when we come up short as Jonah does?

6. How is this consolation confirmed and consolidated in the New Testament?

6

Jonah in the New Testament

For starters

Is it right to be 'proud' of your spiritual heritage?

The book of Jonah has been a significant part of Jewish culture for many centuries. Even today, the reading of the book of Jonah is prescribed for the Day of Atonement, the holiest day of the Jewish calendar and a day of repentance and confession.

The significance of Jonah is also clear in New Testament times. Jesus refers to it in a number of places, notably after being asked for "a sign" by the scribes and Pharisees.

Jesus opposes the desire for a sign; he is not impressed by it. This negative emphasis comes out strongly in Luke's Gospel. There we are told of how Zechariah became dumb for the period of his wife's pregnancy, apparently because of his desire for some validation from God that his word from the angel was true (Lk 1:8-25). In Luke 4:1-13, we are similarly told of the devil's attempt to force Jesus to validate who he was rather than simply live dependently on God and his word.

In the face of sign seeking, Jesus responds by saying that he will refuse all signs except the sign of Jonah. He does this in three passages: Matthew 12:38-42, Matthew 16:1-4, and Luke 11:29-32.

Investigate

Read Matthew 12:38-42 and 16:1-4, and Luke 11:29-32.

1. List the similarities and differences between the three references to Jonah.

Similarities

Differences

2. What are the similarities between the city of Nineveh in Jonah and the generation to which Jesus speaks in these Gospel passages?

The sign of Jonah

Luke 11 tells us that "Jonah became a sign to the people of Nineveh" and that in a similar way the Son of Man will be a sign to "this generation". In Matthew 12, Jesus explains this by more explicitly pointing out the parallel between Jonah being three days and three nights in the belly of a great fish and the Son of Man being three days and three nights in the heart of the earth.

The logic appears to be as follows:
- Although the Ninevites may not have been aware of it, the supreme validation that Jonah was one sent by God to speak the word of God was that he was rescued from death to do it.
- So God will respond to the Jewish request for a sign by validating Jesus through resurrection from the dead.

There is something here that is strangely reminiscent of what we have read previously about the grace of God. As we have seen so often, here in the Gospels God's people request a sign that expresses their lack of belief in God. As such they deserve judgement, like Zechariah in Luke 1. However, in his mercy God responds to their unbelief by the death of his Son, thereby enabling their forgiveness. In other words, God does grant them one more sign and the means whereby their unbelief can be forgiven. This sign is one that they can't afford to miss.

Having replied to their request for a sign, Jesus moves on to speak about repentance.

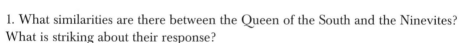

Investigate

Re-read Matthew 12:38-42 and 16:1-4, Luke 11:29-32 and 1 Kings 10:1-13 (cf. 2 Chr 9:1-12).

1. What similarities are there between the Queen of the South and the Ninevites? What is striking about their response?

2. What is Jesus saying that we should learn from the book of Jonah?

Healthy eyes

Although some of our versions put a heading between Luke 11:29-32 and Luke 11:33-36, they can be considered as part of the same speech by Jesus.

In the world of first century Palestine, the eyes were understood differently to how we think of the body. They didn't so much function by allowing light to come in but by allowing the body's own light to go out. In other words, the eye was considered to be a sort of channel or conduit for light, thereby making sight possible. As Jesus expressed it, "Your eye is the lamp of your body".

This ancient view of light and sight was sometimes used in an ethical sense as well. We can see something of this in Deuteronomy 15:9 which describes a person who has an unworthy thought in his heart and whose eye therefore looks grudgingly on his poor fellow Israelite. In other words, what he sees and does is a reflection of what he is like inside. An eye that sees the brother properly is an eye that is healthy and informed by a healthy heart. An eye that sees the brother improperly is an eye that is bad and informed by a bad heart.

In subsequent verses, Jesus warns the Pharisees that their inner life is full of greed and wickedness (Lk 11:39). This is why they cannot see Jesus properly or hear his word properly. Luke 11:35-36 is therefore a challenge to his Jewish hearers. Their inner life testifies to a lack of health that inevitably affects their spiritual eyesight. They need to take a good long look at Jesus, heed the coming sign, and repent like the Ninevites.

The warning is also there for us. At times our inner lives are also full of a similar wickedness that can only be cured by taking a good hard look at Jesus, heeding the sign of Jonah, and repenting with vigour like the Ninevites.

· God

Think it through

1. Summarise what you have learnt from the book of Jonah about…

• Yourself

• The people of God in the Old and New Testament

• God's purpose in this world

2. List five practical and concrete actions you want to take in response to what you have learnt.

3. Share one of these actions with a friend, and ask them to pray that you will carry out this action and help you to pursue it.

4. If you are using this study in a group you might like to share some of these things with each other and spend time praying about them in the group.

MATTHIAS MEDIA

Who are we?

Ever since 'St Matthias Press and Tapes' first opened its doors in 1988, under the auspices of St Matthias Anglican Church, Centennial Park, in Sydney, our aim has been to provide the Christian community with products of a uniformly high standard—both in their biblical faithfulness and in the quality of the writing and production.

Now known as Matthias Media, we have grown to become an international provider of user-friendly resources, with Christians of all sorts using our Bible studies, books, Briefings, audio cassettes, videos, training courses—you name it.

Buy direct from us and save

If you order your Matthias Media resources direct from us, you not only save time and money, you invest in more great resources for the future:

- you save time—we usually despatch our orders within 24 hours of receiving them
- you save money—our normal prices are better than other retailers' discounts (plus if you order in bulk, you'll save even more)
- you help keep us afloat—because we get more from each sale, buying from us direct helps us to stay alive in the difficult world of publishing.

Please call us for a free catalogue of all our resources, including an up-to-date list of other titles in this Interactive Bible Studies series. Or join our email news list from our Web Site. Some details of other IBS titles can be found on page 4.

In Australia, contact Matthias Media:

Ph: 1800 814 360 (Sydney 9663 1478)
Fax: (02) 9663 3265
Email: info@matthiasmedia.com.au
Internet: www.matthiasmedia.com.au

In the UK, contact The Good Book Company:

Ph: (020) 8942 0880
Fax: (020) 8942 0990
Email: admin@thegoodbook.co.uk
Internet: www.thegoodbook.co.uk